Backstreet Boys

THE UNOFFICIAL BOOK

Backstreet Boys

THE UNOFFICIAL • BOOK •

Virgin

First published in 1998 by Virgin Books
an imprint of Virgin Publishing Ltd
332 Ladbroke Grove, London W10 5AH

A catalogue record for this book is available from the British Library

ISBN 0 7535 0277 1

Designed by Stonecastle Graphics Ltd

Edited by Philip de Ste. Croix

Printed and bound by Butler and Tanner Ltd

Contents

Part 1 – Take Five Boys

Orlando, Florida, as anyone lucky enough to visit the place will confirm, is second only to Hollywood as America's home of the stars. Not only can the Sunshine State's famous city boast the celebrity-packed environs of Disney World and Universal Studios, but it now has a brand-new, five-star constellation. The Backstreet Boys have already made their mark on Planet Pop with snappy streetwise songs and five very different personalities – and with two platinum albums to their credit, Brian, Howie D, AJ, Nick and Kev are clearly already a major musical force for the new millennium.

Critics may rank theirs an overnight success, but scratch the surface and you'll find that, as so often happens, the Boys' current superstar status is not the result of luck, but the combination of talent and hard work on the part of a number of people, not just the five guys themselves. And being Orlando-based ensured they were in the right place at the right time when the chance for pop fame finally came.

And stardom for Brian, Howie D, AJ, Nick and Kev is truly world-wide. For Britain, and to an even greater extent mainland Europe, has always had a soft spot for boy bands.

From Wham! through Bros to Take That, East 17 and Worlds Apart, young men with musical ambitions have always done famously in the UK. America's only archetypal boy band of the last decade to have made it big has been New Kids On The Block, of whom more later.

Yet the tide turned in the States with the sad end of leading grunge band Nirvana, a (teen) spirit broken by the death of leader Kurt Cobain.

As that musical door closed, a window opened for clean-cut pop. British bands quickly mounted an invasion of the American charts – Boyzone, 911 and the Spice Girls have all made an impact. But the home-grown talent of the Backstreet Boys has won the day. Let's meet the boys.

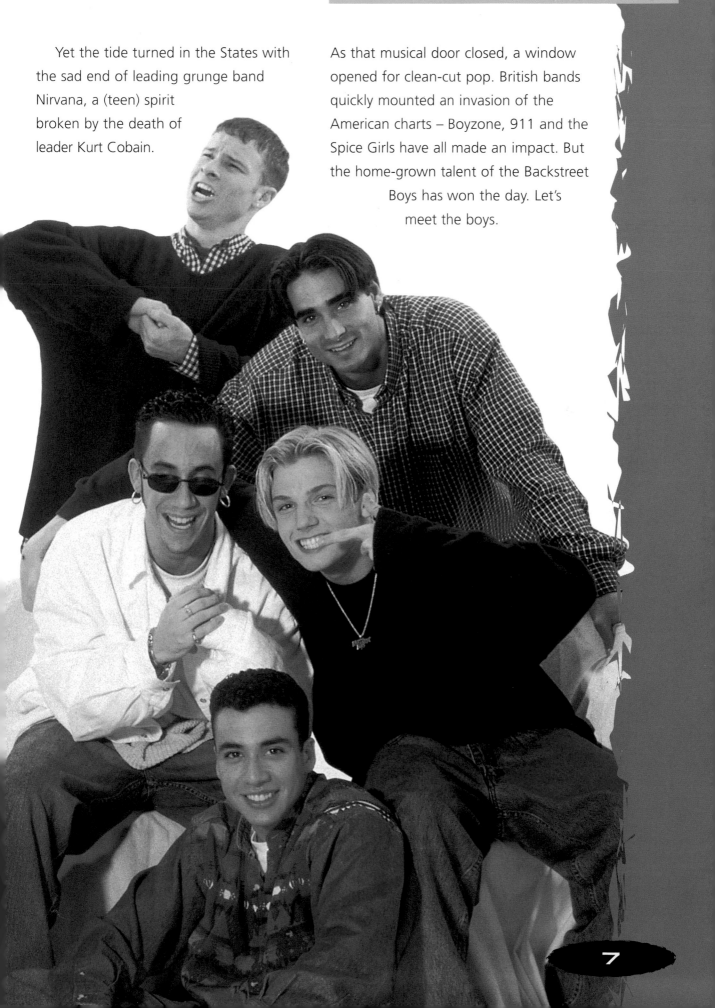

The oldest is Kentucky-born Kevin Richardson, as talented at sitting at a piano as with his vocal chords. It's no coincidence that his two heroes are Elton John and Billy Joel, two famous pianomen themselves. He'd moved to Orlando, disillusioned with his lot playing with a covers band in his native state, to follow a dream of fame and fortune. While he waited, casual work at Walt Disney World paid for his board and lodging: he could be often found dressed up in the guise of Aladdin or a Ninja Turtle. The job wasn't without its hazards: on one occasion, he recalls, his turtle foot flew off while he was performing high-kicks in the Teenage Mutant Ninja Turtle revue. Ever the professional, he went on with the show in his (green) stockinged feet!

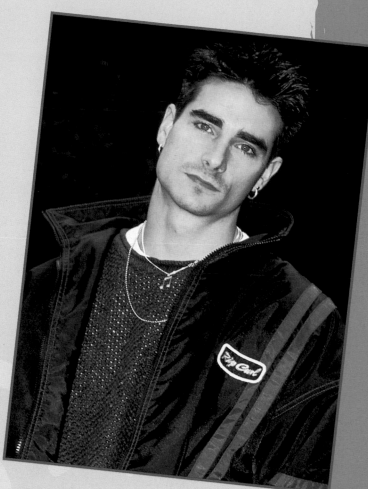

Kevin claims to have had a great childhood, the first nine years of which were spent on a farm. He got his first keyboard in his freshman year of high school and spent his teens singing with a choir and hanging out at drama club. Combining his interests, he entered numerous talent shows and was often invited to play keyboards at restaurants and wedding receptions.

Kev's mother Ann is a sales clerk, while he has two older brothers, Gerald and Tim. Their father, also Gerald, died aged just 49, and watching his health deteriorate over ten months after he was diagnosed with cancer of the colon is something Kevin, understandably, will never get over. His mother and father were high-school sweethearts and the family, as a whole, are very supportive of one another – all of which helped them cope with the effects of the tragedy.

It was his father Gerald who encouraged Kev to go to Orlando to establish a career in music. Until then it looked as if Kev would go into the air force – but armed with his father's blessing he followed his heart rather than take the rational option. The other Boys gave Kevin the nickname Train, because once he gets going there's no stopping him. The father-figure of the group, he admits to being very serious when it comes down to the music and business side of BSB.

Part 1 – Take Five Boys

Howard Dorough, who also goes by the name of Howie D, is a native of Florida. With a Hispanic side to his family, he fancies himself as the most exotic member of the band and eagerly cultivates the image of a Latin lover. This does, however, have a downside as he's inherited curly black hair that is not easily managed. Bad hair days are a frequent occurrence for Howie…and a sure way for the others to wind him up is by tousling his locks!

His mother Paula works in a school, while father Hope, a retired police officer, is now Chief Code Enforcement Officer for Orange County (which means he checks people don't break neighbourhood regulations such as by having overly high fences). He has three sisters and one brother – Angela, Caroline, Polly Anna

and John, all of whom are now in their thirties. It was Polly Anna, an aspiring star herself who reportedly sounds like a cross between Mariah Carey and Gloria Estefan, who first got Howie seriously interested in a career in music.

Howie made his very first bid for musical stardom at the age of three, singing 'Baby Face' on his grandmother's bed – accompanying himself on a toy

Howie made his very first bid for musical stardom at the age of three ...

plastic guitar! These days, you can hear Howie's contribution to BSB in the form of what he describes as his 'high-flying falsetto'. Born in Orlando, the youngest of five half-Irish, half-Puerto Rican children, he's a professionally trained dancer who had worked in community theatre, commercials, TV and appeared in the movies *Parenthood* and *Cop And A Half*, before pop stardom beckoned.

His mother Jackie is a dental secretary, father Harold works in computers and his older brother, aged 24, is called Harold Baker Littrell III. But Harold very nearly ended up an only child: Brian was born with a hole in his heart and, when just five years old, he nearly died of an infection. Having recovered from this near-death experience, his parents were told that that, scientifically speaking, their son should not have survived. He had a temperature of 107° and his heart

Like Kevin, his cousin, Brian Littrell is also from Lexington, Kentucky. Nicknamed B-Rok, he is a huge basketball fan. Musically he's very much into R&B, his favourite artists being soulful crooner Luther Vandross and Boyz II Men, and he admires any other artist with natural talent. The last to join the band, he found their strongly vocal-led, even a cappella, sound suited his musical tastes just fine. Brian's previous working life had seen him taking on a wide variety of jobs, from burger-bar assistant to wedding co-ordinator in a church. He was pulled out of history class in school to take a call from Kevin telling him about the band's audition – the next day found him on a plane to Orlando and boy-band fame!

stopped beating at one point for about 20 seconds. Little wonder Brian is determined to make the most of every single minute now he's back in the land of the living!

Back home in Kentucky, both Kevin and Brian were involved with state and church choirs, as well as the local entertainment scene. They used to sing at family get-togethers, their favourite artists including Boyz II Men, Shai and Jodeci.

Alex 'AJ' McLean was born in Boynton Beach, near Miami, Florida, and he has worked in the entertainment industry since he was six years old. Having brought the house down in his first acting role as Dopey in *Snow White and the Seven Dwarfs*, by sixth grade he'd appeared in 27 classic shows including *The Nutcracker*, *The King And I* and *Fiddler On The Roof*. While at junior high he won a part in Nickelodeon's *Hi Honey, I'm Home*, so beginning a long-running relationship with the Nickelodeon and Disney satellite TV channels.

AJ, who was just 12 years old at the time, first met Howie at a talent contest they'd both entered. AJ won with a 45-minute solo show, carrying away the prize money of $1,000 (which he spent immediately!). Howie was among the first to congratulate him.

An only child – mother Denise and father Bob, both involved in the computer industry, divorced when he was four – AJ cites his uncle as a major influence on his life. He was bass player in a 1950s band called Richie and the Rockets, though,

unlike the Backstreet Boys, the group never made it to the big time.

With Denise employed as the group's on-the-road publicist-cum-tour manager, AJ sees much more of his mother than the other guys do of theirs. But her presence doesn't seem to have stopped this boy from showing off. He has probably the most striking image among the band members, and is known for his tattoos, constant experimentation with his hair colour and a liking for cool shades. A self-confessed ham, he loves the limelight and can't help doing crazy stuff for no apparent reason – especially on stage. As proof, he recently appeared on stage as *Batman* baddie the Riddler, dressed in a green Spandex outfit: the audience went wild while his colleagues looked on in disbelief! According to the rest of the band he is also the 'funniest drunk', but we'll draw a veil over that!

Nick Carter, the youngest of the famous five, is fully seven years younger than Kevin and the only Boy to be born in the 1980s – yet from the outset his abundant talent has meant his relative youth has been overlooked, at least in musical terms. As a young child-actor he appeared in a TV series called *Club Kids* and at the age of eight he landed a part in the Andrew Lloyd Webber stage musical *Phantom Of The Opera*.

Currently over six feet tall and still growing, Nick is the tallest band member – some would also say the clumsiest – but is also the fans' favourite. Luckily, this doesn't cause a problem for the rest of the Boys. When the group formed it was accepted that one or two of them would inevitably get more fan and media attention than the others, and it's all considered to be for the greater good of the band as a whole.

A self-confessed ham, he loves the limelight and can't help doing crazy stuff for no apparent reason . . .

The downside for Nick of being such a fresh-faced, blue-eyed boy is that he hasn't been old enough to drink or go clubbing with the rest of BSB and has had to stay in his hotel room playing Nintendo! He used to get teased a lot by the others because he was the baby of the bunch, but that doesn't happen so much since his latest growth spurt. He actually quite likes being the youngest, and the attention it generates.

With his sun-kissed blond locks, Nick looks like a surfing dude…but in reality he is a licensed scuba diver. (Well, it had to be something fishy!) He has probably the widest musical tastes of the five and, as well as being a huge Oasis fan, also listens to – deep breath – AC/DC, Bone Thugs 'N' Harmony, Kriss Kross, Prince, Tom Petty, R-Kelly, Jodeci, N-Trance, Lenny Kravitz, Mary J Blige and Nirvana (phew!). Nick has always fantasized about being a pop star and is a firm believer in the American dream – the idea that you can accomplish whatever you set your mind to do.

Nick's mother Jane and father Robert used to run a retirement home. He has four younger siblings: twins Aaron and Ang, Lesley and BJ. Lesley is a teenage model (that height gene coming into play again), while little brother Aaron is already enjoying success in his own musical career. Having formed his own band at eight years old called Dead End, Aaron recently signed a solo recording deal in Germany. He had a UK hit single, 'Crush On You', in December 1997, and also joined BSB on stage when the band played Berlin.

So how did the five get together? Credit for the concept of the Backstreet Boys goes to one Lou J Pearlman, cousin of Art Garfunkel – he of 'Bridge Over Troubled Water' fame and the taller half of the duo Simon and Garfunkel. Lou is now their business manager and helps run the BSB company in which the boys have an equal fifth share.

He brought in the management team of Donna and Johnny Wright, the partnership that thrust 1990 chart-toppers New Kids On The Block into the limelight, to help turn his dream into musical reality. They held auditions for attractive, young male hopefuls to form a group to record for their label, but even their expectations were exceeded when the five Backstreet Boys were discovered.

Rather like the Spice Girls, the future members of BSB had been hanging out in the same showbiz circles for some time. Although not yet best buddies, the 'wannabes' had certainly made one another's acquaintance when the idea of a band was still just a twinkle in Lou Pearlman's eye. Nick had met AJ and Howie at acting auditions; they had filled slack time while waiting to be called by singing Temptations hits or songs they'd just heard on the radio.

The trio then saw the Wrights' newspaper advertisement and promptly applied. So did Kevin and his cousin Brian. Even at this stage, Kevin had already been told by a colleague at Disney about 'those guys who harmonize all the time'. The seeds of success had been sown, the five were brought together and Backstreet Boys was created.

Since that time, of course, the guys have become good mates. Miraculously, especially when you consider the amount

of time they spend together on the road, Howie, Brian and Kev decided to share an appartment back in Florida. Brian has subsequently moved out to share a place with AJ, though this is not thought to be the result of any falling-out.

Brian and Nick have become the best of friends, despite the five-year age gap. Brian describes his pal as the little brother he never had (though maybe little isn't the best word to describe Nick these days!). They have been given the nicknames Frick and Frack because they are always to be found together, the pair who mess around and consequently get told off by 'serious' Kev. Brian considers Nick to be very mature for his age and doubts whether he himself would have managed to cope so well with the BSB phenomenon had he been Nick's age.

Happily, Nick has just as much respect for his fellow band members. Explaining that the guys are the only real friends he has, Kevin likens the whole group to a family of close brothers. Apparently there are occasional fights, but certainly nothing the average family doesn't also go through. When fights blow up, it's Howie, the mediator, who tends to sort them out.

The seeds of success had been sown, the five were brought together and Backstreet Boys was created ...

Of the others, Nick is the practical joker, Kevin the down-to-business figurehead, AJ the romantic flirt and Brian the shy guy. Look out, though, for his uncannily accurate Jim Carrey impersonation... because with Backstreet Boys it's smiles all the way!

Nick Carter

Full name: Nicholas Gene Carter

Date of birth: 28 January 1980 (Aquarius)

Place of birth: Jamestown, New York

Nickname: Nick

Height: 6ft 1in

Weight: 140 pounds

Eyes: Blue

Hair: Blond

Hero: Ridley Scott (film director)

Heroines: Cindy Crawford and Sharon Stone

Hobby: Nintendo

Favourite Food: Pizza

Favourite drink: Cola

Favourite colour: Green

Secret: Amazingly, given his current six-foot stature, Nick was bullied at school for having time off for acting assignments. Later he had his own private tutor on tour.

havin
mem
relati
have
more
lives.
fanc
awa
Kent
true
him
his

rem
him
fore

Love And Romance

A couple of the guys have had serious relationships in the past. Kevin was engaged to a girl called Beth when just 19 but, realizing they were both too young for marriage, the couple split up. He explains that the band have just been so busy travelling that it's been impossible to maintain a relationship up until now.

Kev, like Nick, doesn't let any potential girlfriend know what he does when they first meet. He usually says he's a businessman or has some other (non-starring) role in the entertainment industry, not wishing to come across as arrogant. He claims he wouldn't get jealous if another guy looked at his girl,

but would consider it a compliment. However, he wouldn't take so kindly to her flirting or playing games, and if that happened he would call it a day. (You could write a song about that: does 'Quit Playin' Games…' sound familiar?)

Inevitably, as the oldest BSB, Kev has seen many of his friends back home get married and even start families. To show he might one day make a fine father, he has a two-year-old goddaughter called Madison, whom he tries to see as often as possible when he goes home. He is at the stage now when he would dearly like to be in a relationship and is on the lookout for that special someone. And

He claims he wouldn't get jealous if another guy looked at his girl, but would consider it a compliment.

who knows how old she'll be? Kev attracts older fans and has received mail from women – not girls – in their thirties and forties!

AJ, who has a reputation for being a ladykiller, always gets on well with girls – something he puts down to growing up in a female household with his mother

and grandmother. At school, though, he didn't fit in with the rest of the boys, whose life centred around the decidedly macho pursuits of basketball, football, fights and gangs. Anyone with aspirations to be a singer or dancer was considered downright weird. Mind you, he also used to borrow and wear his mother's clip-on earrings before he had his ears pierced – so he was asking for trouble! As a consequence he used to stay at the back of the class chatting with – and chatting up – the ladies.

His first crush, in fact, happened in the classroom and the object of his affections was his fourth-grade teacher, Miss Olney. He tried to be the best student he could for her, but didn't mind the couple of detentions he received – because then he had her undivided attention!

the contrary, he believes they should view it as a challenge!

AJ has never been turned down when asking a girl on a date and is, apparently, attracted to girls with attitude – girls who, according to him, are quite shy when they're not with their mates. His one fault is that he has a tendency to be over-protective, a jealous flaw that's lost him two girlfriends. This hasn't put him off, though, and he's always on the lookout for the perfect love-match he believes is waiting out there for everyone.

Brian might not agree: he apparently

AJ still dates an ex-girlfriend, Marisa, when he goes home, considering her to be his best friend; she's even accompanied him on tour. In the past, he also had a two-year relationship with a girl called Jennifer. Not surprisingly, he is considered to be a bit of a romantic and out of all the Boys he is the best at communicating with girls. He has his own aspirations as far as the ladies are concerned and reportedly wants to do a show with chart-toppers No Doubt because he's fallen head over heels for lead singer Gwen Stefani! She's apparently everything he ever wants in a woman and he can't stop talking about her. AJ doesn't think that BSB having girlfriends should put the fans off – on hasn't been in a relationship for over two years now! According to the other band members, though, he's a real attention-seeker and, while AJ will start a conversation with a girl, it's Bri who will end up getting all the attention…He rates a number of famous babes and once waited outside Tower Records in London in a bid to see what Mariah Carey looked like in the flesh! His favourite famous ladies are Pamela Anderson, Sandra Bullock and his favourite Spice is the extrovert Scary – Mel B. Brian confides that if he had a girlfriend he wouldn't keep her a secret – far from it! He'd be open about his relationship, maintaining that the band don't have rules like that.

Considering his reputation as a Latin lover, Howie tends to keep the details of his love life very close to his chest. Although he doesn't reveal much to the press, he reportedly tells his family everything. He gets advice on girls from his brother Johnny. Other than that, he wants a huge Catholic wedding and three kids, but there's little further information on his search for that prospective wife and mother. Keep 'em guessing, Howie…

Part 2 – Down To Work

Having decided on a name inspired by the Backstreet Market, a famous Orlando landmark, it was time for the band to get down to work. Initial marketing campaigns included sampler cassettes distributed in Bantam's teenage-targeted *Love Stories* series of books and JC Penney's Kaboodles make-up cases. Even at this early stage it was obvious that their attraction to the male market would be limited – not that the Boys have ever complained about their predominantly female following!

In the early days, the fame-hungry five would sing practically anywhere. Howie recalls performing a cappella in the foyer of the offices of local record labels to get noticed. Within six months, they were one of the top live bands in Florida – prepared to play any venue, from school gymnasiums to Sea World. They developed a ritual before going on stage – they'd stand in a circle and pray, stretch and loosen up, then finally wish each other good luck.

And luck was certainly going to be needed as they entered the crowded showbiz arena. They released 'Tell Me That I'm Dreaming' on their management's independent Transcontinental label in a bid to generate further exposure and attract interest from one of the major record companies. But it was the age-old story – natural talent is all very well, but to hit the big time you need some major

financial muscle behind you. And that, inevitably, comes in the form of a big record company.

This was where manager Donna Wright stepped in. She had been pleading with her friend David McPherson of Jive Records to go along to a gig and hear the band. He never seemed to have the time, so Donna rang him from her mobile phone at one of their concerts, held the handset away from her ear and simply let him hear the noise the fans were making. That did the trick, and the Backstreet Boys were signed immediately.

They spent some time laying down tracks in the recording studio before hitting the road, leaving behind three classic singles for release: 'We've Got It Goin' On', 'I'll Never Break Your Heart' and 'Roll With It' (any similarity to the Oasis track stops at the title). The five visited Europe for the first time in the summer of 1995, touring with TV-promoted duo PJ and Duncan, and made their mark straight away.

Although 'We've Got It Goin' On' only reached Number 54 in the UK charts when first released (Number 69 in the *Billboard* US listing), *Smash Hits* – the trendsetting 'Bible of pop' – saw its potential. They gave the debut single no fewer than five stars and, thanks to extensive coverage, its readers voted Backstreet Boys Newcomers of the Year in their annual poll. It was just a case of waiting for record buyers to pick up on the vibe.

'We've Got It Goin' On' had been re-released for a second bite of the cherry in August 1996. This time it achieved its deserved hit status, peaking at Number 3.

Following this success, the second single 'I'll Never Break Your Heart' was re-issued, received substantial radio airplay and scaled the UK charts to reach Number 8, giving them two major hits within three months.

The only glitch in the Boys' smooth progress towards worldwide pop domination came when Kev came down with appendicitis, requiring an immediate operation. Forget the Spice Girls' '2 Become 1'… the Backstreet Boys' five had to become four for a while! Understandably homesick while confined to bed in a German hospital, Kev recuperated on his own while the show went on for the remaining band members. The band and Kev bounced back, though, none the worse for the experience…with the exception of a couple of operation scars below the waistline which Kev isn't inclined to show to just *anybody*!

The debut album was released in September 1996, making it into the UK Top 20 at the first time of asking. Taking their name as its title, it included a track 'Boys Will Be Boys', which could easily have been their theme tune. It was, in fact, used on the soundtrack of Eddie Murphy's film *The Nutty Professor*, further spreading the BSB word.

With two Number 3 hit singles to their credit, much was expected of 'Quit Playin' Games (With My Heart)' which, released at the very start of 1997, shot up the charts like a rocket. Ironically, BSB were kept off the top spot in the UK only by fellow American Tori Amos, leaving their latest hit nestling at Number 2 behind her song 'Professional Widow'. Next to hit the chart heights was 'Anywhere For You', a two-year-old track released in March to claim fourth position.

Having experienced life with both an independent and a major record label, and having put almost as much time into publicity interviews as performing on the road, it's fair to say the Boys have learnt a fair amount about the music business *en route*. Their interest in their industry extends beyond simply making music; both Kev and Brian list *Hit Men* by Frederick Dannen among their favourite

'Quit Playin' Games (With My Heart)'... shot up the charts like a rocket.

reads. (The book is an honest, factual account of the American music industry which uncovers its early Mafia connections and provides some valuable information on career pitfalls to avoid.) Brian believes Dannen gives a good background insight and warns of things that people would never tell you directly. He accepts that there are sides to the business that he doesn't like, but these are more that compensated for by the aspect he loves – performing and recording his music!

As groups like Bros have found out to their cost in the past, ignorance isn't always bliss in the music industry. If the Boys keep their wits about them, they will have something substantial to show for their time as BSB, even when the band eventually has to call it a day. They have their own company and are fully responsible for planning their tours, making sure the budget balances as well as taking care of the creative aspects. They admit that a large entourage is necessary when they hit the road, including security personnel (one bodyguard for each Boy because the fans are so clever at tracking them down), stylists and the rest, but stress that everyone has a job to do and there are no hangers-on. All five

seem to appreciate the value of money, without being motivated by greed.

Apart from the financial rewards, being a pop star can bring some juicy perks. Lunches at Arnold Schwarzenegger's Los Angeles branch of Planet Hollywood and free scooters from Honda are certainly appreciated, although one member of the group did say they'd really like a convertible Mercedes like the five the Spice Girls have apparently received! And how do the boys spend their own hard-earned money? It ranges from Nick's Nintendo games to cars, jeeps and the jewellery for which the boys are well-known.

Brian recently bought a necklace worth $2,000 (equivalent to £1,250), a thick

chain bearing a diamond-encrusted cross, which he protects with his life. When on tour in Sydney, Australia, he had a gold necklace made that spelled out his nickname B-Rok, while all five received BSB pendants from their management company as recognition of their hard work and commitment. AJ seems to be hankering after a home of his own. He has his eye on a house in Orlando, but

...being a pop star can bring some juicy perks...

also quite fancies the idea of owning an English castle. Such are the fruits of success...

Howie Dorough

Full name:
Howard Dwayne Dorough

Date of birth:
22 August 1973 (Leo)

Place of birth:
Orlando, Florida

Nickname: Howie D

Height: 5ft 6in

Weight: 133 pounds

Eyes: Brown

Hair: Black

Hero: His father

Heroine: Cindy Crawford

Hobby: Water skiing

Favourite Food:
Chinese

Favourite drink:
Sprite

Favourite smell: Cool Water

Favourite Film:
Willy Wonka And The Chocolate Factory

Secret:
He auditioned under the stage name of Tony Donetti – but didn't get called back straightaway because the management lost his address! Six months later, it resurfaced and he got the job.

Home Is Where The Heart Is

The Boys have certainly travelled throughout the world, although it's debatable how much they actually got to see because of their packed schedule – not to mention security considerations. Inevitably much of their time is spent at concert venues, in hotel rooms and visiting record shops to make personal appearances. When the publicity machine kicks in with a diary-full of photo shoots, PAs and interviews for the media, it leaves little time for sightseeing. Often the occasional days pencilled in as 'days off' are actually spent travelling to the next gig.

As Howie explains, they always try to see the sights when visiting a new country for the first time, but more often than not they only get to see their hotel and the arena where they're performing. They do, at least, get to meet the people and

Howie has learned first-hand how the melting pot of cultures that makes up the US today came about as a result of people emigrating from Europe many years ago.

In the first year or two, the Boys' efforts – and consequently their success – were concentrated on Europe. Germany always seems to have had a soft spot for boy bands, maybe a throwback to the Beatles' early days in Hamburg. BSB have appeared on the cover of every teen mag out there, have overtaken Take That in terms of record sales and are more popular than Ireland's Boyzone. It was in Germany that the Backstreet Boys' debut album first achieved platinum status: outside the States, it sold a total of five-and-a-half million copies.

The Boys are regularly mobbed by fans when on tour in Spain and France. Always fond of the limelight, AJ loves the sound their audiences make: he says the noise makes him dizzy and that it's an amazing feeling to know the fans are screaming for them. Somewhat less happily Kev recalls one occasion in Spain when a manic fan ripped his necklace off him after a live radio show. It was a Christmas present from his brother which, understandably, he was upset to lose.

Home Is Where The Heart Is

British fans will be sad, if not surprised, to hear the Boys admit they tend to spend more time in Germany and other European countries than in the UK. It's simply a case of going where the demand is, so if you want to see more of BSB in future years, get everyone you know (and their friends) to buy their releases!

Fans in some countries are a bit 'naughty', displaying rather suggestive signs and banners at the Boys' gigs. Nick admits to being a bit embarrassed by this kind of attention, but quite enjoys the tussling involved in getting in and out of hotels and venues. Which is just as well: the other guys sometimes use their big buddy as a decoy, pushing him first into

the waiting throng so they can sneak out of the tour bus unmolested!

Most of the time the fans are very generous, although the Boys have learned the hard way that you *can* get too much of a good thing. Howie once said he liked Gummi Bears but, having since received thousands, he's now heartily sick of 'em! The fans also have a sense of humour: AJ recalls being hit in the crotch on stage by a banana wearing a pair of sunglasses. He couldn't sing for laughing…

Kevin measures their popularity by the intensity of the reception they get at the airports at each country. In Germany there will be an overwhelming crowd and with their popularity now spreading as far afield as Thailand and the Czech Republic, arrivals are never disappointing.

Despite a heavy touring schedule over the past couple of years, the Boys are still committed to staying on the road and taking their music to the fans. They have a lot of respect for performers like Madonna and Prince, icons of the 1980s who put in their time on the road creating spectacular live performances, and who have become megastars of the 1990s as a result of their hard work. Sometimes BSB have to be up at 4am to get on the road, and there are always promotions and interviews to fit in.

By the autumn of 1996 the Boys were carrying their sound to Asia, the Pacific Rim and Australia. Nick and Brian especially loved the laid-back beach lifestyle of Brisbane, Australia. The weather had its obvious attractions, and the atmosphere was far more relaxed than in most cities. Return visits were swiftly inked in, and these territories are now solidly behind the famous five. But east, west, home's best, as the saying goes, and there's nothing they like better than

Outside Europe, the next place to contract BSB fever was Canada, firstly the eastern French seaboard – as word spread from France – and then the rest of the country. The Canadians are reportedly the Boys' most aggressive fans: so much so that AJ ended up on crutches in a bid to escape the crazed Canucks! His foot was accidentally crushed while he was trying to get away from a throng of fans and he ended up having to hobble around stage in plaster. The album went six times platinum and reached Number 1 in the Canadian charts, while tickets for the 32 shows they were playing there sold out in 20 minutes flat!

landing back in Florida for a bit of well-earned rest and recuperation.

Christmas 1997 was the first for three years that the Boys were able to spend at home. Next on the itinerary was a series of US concert dates as they concentrated on succeeding on home turf. Brian, who tends to miss America most when they're on the road, explained that, although it's exciting to perform to people all over the world, they always wanted to bring their sound home to the States.

American fans are as keen as any and BSB hysteria has hit: fans have found out Howie's home address and started camping out on his mother's lawn! On Mother's Day they brought her flowers and chocolates and, in return, she invited them in for dinner. Fans also write to Howie's parents, and they write back letters to let them know Howie's news and how BSB are getting on. It looks like a case of home sweet home in 1998… and beyond!

Brian Littrell

Full name: Brian Thomas Littrell

Date of birth:
20 February 1975 (Pisces)

Place of birth:
Lexington, Kentucky

Nickname: B-Rok

Height: 5ft 8in

Weight: 140 pounds

Eyes: Blue

Hair: Brown

Heroes:
Boyz II Men and Luther Vandross

Heroine: Pamela Anderson

Hobby: Basketball

Favourite Food: Macaroni

Favourite drink: Iced tea

Favourite smell:
Lagerfeld's Photo

Biggest Fear: Heights

Secret:
Six months before he joined the band,
Brian got a taste of stardom when his
duet with a fellow high-school pupil in a
talent show brought the house down.

Battle OF The Boy Bands

During their short time at the top, the Boys have worked with and met a number of their musical contemporaries. Not only have comparisons been drawn with the likes of Boyzone, 911 and Take That, but also with New Kids On The Block, the early 1990s hitmakers with whom they share a management team.

Okay, they're American, there are five of them and they've both had hits, while Kev's occasional nickname Kevvy Kev, is similar to Marky Mark (the rapper who went on to model underclothes for Calvin Klein) whose brother Donnie Wahlberg was a New Kid. But these are tenuous links at best: the media like nothing more than comparing bands to acts which have gone before, but Backstreet Boys have their own distinctive sound and their own musical ideas.

When confusion *does* arise, then laughter is the best solution. And there were smiles all round when two of the Boys were mistaken for members of another boy band, East 17 – Brian and AJ were confused with Brian and John. Obviously the Boys couldn't have opened their mouths, since they don't sound like they're from Walthamstow! The BSB guys

happily signed autographs (presumably as their real selves!) and moved on.

One thing the Boys do have in common with other groups is a joker in the pack. The prankster in Nick comes out when the Boys hit the road. He once put a sock, stuffed with an assortment of unsavoury, smelly odds'n'ends, behind the drum kit. The stench was, by all accounts, pretty ripe...and retribution has been promised!

In the early days, Backstreet Boys used to wear similar outfits in an attempt to be identified as a band. As they have become a household name, they've been allowed more freedom to express their own individual style and personality, and their looks have inevitably changed. AJ is

...but Backstreet Boys have their own distinctive sound and their own musical ideas ...

now trying to get away from his dark 'shades' image, which is good news for female fans. It's strange that he considers his eyes to be his most attractive feature, yet hides them behind sunglasses! His latest fashion fetish is hats.

Both AJ and Howie have tattoos. When AJ first got his, the Boys' management reportedly gave him a 'slap on the wrist', fearing it would alienate the fans. In fact it had no adverse effect for the band and, in his defence, AJ explained that BSB was never about image. Brian considers their image reflects exactly who they are, and there is room for all types and styles of band in the business.

The Boys appreciate that their looks have contributed to their success and helped generate initial interest – yet they feel they would still have made it to the top on the strength of their music, even if success might have taken a little longer. They are obviously flattered that people like the way they look, but scratch the surface and you find true gold underneath in their voices.

As some of the nicest boys in pop, who keep their feet on the ground thanks to the support of their families, management and one another, they tend to get on with all the other stars they meet and don't have a bad word to say about any of them. It also appears that other bands rate the Boys – indeed 911, a band their own age who often attend BSB gigs, cited them as one of their main influences. The guys claimed to be really touched by that 'mind-blowing' accolade from their contemporaries.

The Boys recently played a celebrity basketball game with 'N Sync in Berlin, scotching persistent rumours that the two groups (who share their management team) do not get on. The guys maintain they haven't spent enough time with them to have an opinion either way. They are all friendly with Boyzone, whom they tend to bump into quite a lot, 3T and Peter Andre. They go to the 'Zone's gigs and Boyzone show up at BSB concerts whenever they're able to. Australian Peter Andre is liked by all the guys, who rate him a good all-round performer with an excellent voice.

They also shared a dressing room in Germany with the Spice Girls, reportedly at the girls' own insistence. The BSB verdict: cool and friendly! On the subject of dressing rooms, the lads once threw Nick out of theirs into a throng of awaiting fans, dressed in just his underpants. And that's the naked truth…

Battle Of The Boy Bands

When they were in LA recently to shoot a video, they met up with a whole cluster of bands all staying in the same hotel, and all shooting their own videos. The guest list included Quad City DJs, Dru Hill, Joe, Blackstreet, Salt'n'Pepa and LL Cool J. AJ especially rates Dru Hill. His own sound has been likened to that group's Sisqo, which he considers a real compliment.

Although they are aware that they appeal specifically to a younger female audience, BSB just concentrate on the music and leave the marketing to their record company. They believe that the strength of their live performances and natural talent will see them through and prove they are much more than just good-lookers.

Unlike many of their musical contemporaries, Backstreet Boys don't rely on engineered sounds or instruments: it is their vocal ability alone that creates the right mood and magic.

Their sound has also changed since they first came on the scene. Sometimes this has happened more through the force of circumstance than because of intentional decisions. AJ's most recent rendition of 'Lay Down Beside Me' is two whole octaves lower than on the original version, as his voice has deepened and he's no longer able to reach the high notes!

Brian recalls that Europe provided a ready-made market for BSB as they

already were experiencing the boy-band phenomenon. He claims that, as Americans, they brought a fresh sound to Europe – one that had an edge. Unlike some of the boy bands already around, they weren't just pretty faces…they could actually sing. What's more, each member of the band has his own sound.

Kevin admits to being jealous of AJ's raspy soul-funk voice and Brian's smooth Kenny 'Footloose' Loggins style. As a general rule, the guys are not keen on being referred to as a 'boy band'; they don't like to be pigeonholed. But they accept that for the moment it is inevitable and understand how people (especially media people) like to categorize a sound, look or age group.

Clever marketing and publicity can give any image-led band exposure, but it's only talent that can keep them at the top. Given time, BSB will prove to the world that they are much more than five pretty faces.

AJ McLean

Full name: Alexander James McLean

Date of birth:
9 January 1978 (Capricorn)

Place of birth:
Boynton Beach, Florida

Nickname: AJ

Height: 5ft 9in

Weight: 126 pounds

Eyes: Brown

Hair: Black

Hero: His uncle

Heroine: Cindy Crawford

Hobby: Swimming

Favourite Food:
McDonald's

Favourite drink:
Mountain Dew

Favourite smell: CK One

**Favourite school
subject:** English

Odd jobs: Ventriloquist

Secret:
He may be a babe magnet these days, but
AJ admits his very first girlfriend dumped
him because he told lies!

Part 3 – BSB Conquer The World

It took a long coming, but the Backstreet Boys are finally achieving their dream of US recognition. Back in 1995 when they first released 'We've Got It Goin' On' in the States, the charts were very much grunge-orientated. Howie, in particular, feels the mood of the nation wasn't ready yet for their R&B-influenced pop.

Now that time has finally come, and they've been concentrating their effort on their homeland – while appreciating that some of their European fans, who have always been behind the group, may feel a bit neglected. The boys are careful not to take their supporters for granted, realizing how important they are to the group's survival. They try to give them special attention and occasionally even ring some lucky fan – though most of the time the girl they're calling refuses to believe she's actually speaking to a Backstreet Boy!

As their popularity has grown and their schedule remains as packed as ever, the Boys have had to spread themselves ever more thinly. But they hope their followers will understand. As AJ says, you can't get caught up with it as there is no way to please everybody. Brian thinks of the fans as part of the extended BSB family and is sad the band members can't spend as much time as they'd like with them. He wants them all to rest assured that they are not forgotten.

The early part of 1997 was spent in studios recording their all-important second album with which they planned to consolidate their initial impact. They were also preparing to win over their fellow countrymen. Nick re-asserted that they always wanted to bring their music home, but needed to ensure that the BSB magic was at full strength to make it.

In Summer 1997 the Boys had a whole ten days off – their first proper holiday for a year and a half. Kevin stayed put in Orlando, explaining that he spends enough time travelling when on tour. The rest of the guys went their separate ways with friends and family. They then spent

Brian thinks of the fans as part of the extended BSB family...

some time in Miami filming in a shopping mall. Brian recalls that no one there seemed to bat an eyelid and they enjoyed walking around without security, just like five regular guys. They all looked forward to breaking into the American market and found the opportunity of starting all over again really exciting.

Part 3 – BSB Conquer The World

But the chance of walking around in blissful anonymity didn't last long, as they found themselves well on their way to becoming a household name Stateside. 'Quit Playin' Games (With My Heart)' sold more than a million copies in the US and entered the *Billboard* Top 5, while the first album, only recently released in America, went gold, selling more than half a million.

In a bid to keep both Europe and the Americas happy, the Boys' second album, 'Backstreet's Back' (recorded in Sweden, Britain and America, and, like the debut, featuring a bewildering variety of different producers and songwriters) was released in Europe in August, at the same time as the re-packaged first album hit the shelves in the US. The second album was launched with a TV broadcast from Times Square in New York beamed live across the world by satellite.

All the musical bases were covered, with 'Like A Child' even featuring strings in the orchestration. Another ballad, a cover of PM Dawn's 1991 hit 'Set Adrift On Memory Bliss', based on Spandau Ballet's song 'True', was produced by the hip-hop act themselves. Another famed writing and production team, Full Force, came through with the funky 'All I Have To Give'. All in all, it was an impressive musical step forward with at least five potential Top 10 singles waiting to follow the opening pair of cuts, 'Everybody' and 'As Long As You Love Me', up the charts.

The period from early December '97 to early February '98 (with the exception of Christmas) was spent touring Canada and the USA. The BSB schedule was already booked solid up to summer '98, taking in Germany, Chile, New York, France and Ireland. England was scheduled for a visit in mid- to late March, while next came Scandinavia and Northern Europe and then a trip down to Spain before returning to the US.

So what of the future for the Boys? Looking forward to the end of the decade, they all want to remain with and continue to develop the group. No-one is currently admitting to ambitions for a solo career. Each member is an integral part of the whole, and the view is that if one leaves – God forbid – there will be no band. They don't see a problem in staying as they are, and don't feel inclined to change the name Backstreet Boys to Backstreet Men. Like those American music legends the Beach Boys, they feel they can hang on to their name as they get older. If that view changes, there is always the option of dropping Boys to become simply Backstreet.

The five are also all keen on the idea of breaking into movies in the future. Their pasts were not restricted to the music industry and they see no reason why their futures should be. But for the time being, they emphasize that they are happy to concentrate on the group and write more of their own songs (Brian wrote the sumptuous 'That's What She Said' on the new album). Howie is currently learning the guitar with the aim of playing live on stage on their next big tour. There has been talk of a Backstreet Boys movie,

possibly along the lines of *Spiceworld*, but the idea remains just talk for the moment. Brian would ultimately like to be a comedy film actor in the style of his idol Jim Carrey, while Howie, with a background in films, would also like to combine his musical talents with a movie career.

Having been starved on the relationship front due to their schedule of the past few years, not surprisingly all the guys will be on the lookout for that certain someone special.

In line with the spirit of the American Dream, the Backstreet Boys look set to accomplish all their goals, and their fans will no doubt enjoy their adventures along the way. Boys will be boys – and don't we just love it!

The five are also all keen on the idea of breaking into movies in the future.

Kevin Richardson

Full name: Kevin Richardson

Date of birth:
3 October 1972 (Libra)

Place of birth:
Lexington, Kentucky

Nickname: Kev or Kevvy Kev

Height: 6ft 1in

Weight: 175 pounds

Eyes: Green

Hair: Black

Heroes:
Elton John and Billy Joel

Heroine: Michelle Pfeiffer

Hobby: Basketball

Favourite food:
Mexican

Favourite smell:
Paco Rabanne XS

Favourite colour:
Royal blue

Secret:
Kev harboured a dream of being a fighter pilot after seeing Tom Cruise in *Top Gun* – but the Air Force wouldn't let him postpone his training so he chose music instead.

Awards And Successes

In their musical career to date, the Boys have enjoyed amazing chart success across the globe and scooped up awards by the armful. The *Smash Hits* award for Best Newcomers of '95 evidently started the ball rolling, and the magazine still remains intensely loyal to the Boys. In December 1997 the five took away five more *Smash Hits* awards – one for each mantelpiece! – all voted for by the readers.

In between times, in November '96, came the accolade of being voted Most Popular Band in Europe at the MTV European Music Awards, beating off heavy competition in the form of Oasis, the Spice Girls and Jamiroquai. The award was presented to them by former Take That star Robbie Williams, now enjoying more than a little success in his solo career. In his acceptance speech, Brian paid tribute to his uncle (Kev's father),

thanking all the Boys' family and friends whether watching at home or 'up above'.

The same year saw the Boys voted Best International Group by German TV viewers. Their single 'I'll Never Break Your Heart' went gold there and topped the charts in neighbouring Austria. Incidentally both Brian and Kevin were so overcome with emotion when they received their first gold record that tears were shed…but the Boys have now gone multi-platinum in 16 countries and sold over eight million records worldwide. They've also had six Top 10 singles in Britain alone while their long-play video has gone ten times platinum in Canada.

That board-sweeping performance at the *Smash Hits* Awards, walking away with five trophies, is worth further reflection. Prizes were awarded for Best Album and Best Album Cover for 'Backstreet's Back', Best Video for

'Everybody' (which AJ considers to be the band's turning point in the quest for superstardom) and 'Best International Band'. The fifth award – and surely the most coveted – went to Nick for Best Male Haircut.

A capacity audience of 10,000 attended the ceremony at London Arena with a contingent of Backstreet fans making their presence felt in no uncertain way. By comparison, the likes of Peter Andre and the Spice Girls received a fairly subdued response from the crowd. The tabloid press all duly noted how the Boys overshadowed the heroines of Girl Power and received a standing ovation into the bargain.

For the second year running, the Boys also won MTV Europe's coveted *Select* Award. Described as the ultimate viewers' choice, *Select* is MTV Europe's daily jukebox show where viewers request their favourite video from an on-screen menu – and 'As Long As You Love Me' beat songs from the Spices, Hanson and Puff Daddy. So, as the accolades, awards and gold records continue to come piling in and each new release continues to climb charts across the globe, the future for the Backstreet Boys certainly looks bright – those gold and platinum discs shimmering just as brightly as the guys' jewellery!

UK & US Discography

Singles

'We've Got It Goin' On'
Released UK: October 1995/Released US: October 1995
Highest UK chart position: 54/Highest US chart position: 69

'I'll Never Break Your Heart'
Released UK: December 1995/Not released in US
Highest UK chart position: 42

'Get Down (You're The One For Me)'
Released UK: May 1996/Not released in US
Highest UK chart position: 14

'We've Got It Goin' On'
Re-released UK: August 1996
Highest UK chart position: 3

'I'll Never Break Your Heart'
Re-released UK: November 1996/Not released in US
Highest UK chart position: 8

'Quit Playin' Games (With My Heart)'
Released UK: January 1997/Released US: June 1997
Highest UK chart position: 2/Highest US chart position: 2

'Anywhere For You'
Released UK: March 1997/Not released in US
Highest UK chart position: 4

'Everybody (Backstreet's Back)'
Released UK: August 1997/Not released in US
Highest UK chart position: 3

'As Long As You Love Me'
Released UK: September 1997/Currently at radio in US
Highest UK chart position: 3

Albums

'Backstreet Boys'
Released UK: September 1996
Highest UK chart position: 12
We've Got It Goin' On/Anywhere For You/Get Down (You're The One For Me)/I'll Never Break Your Heart/Quit Playin' Games (With My Heart)/Boys Will Be Boys/Just To Be Close To You/I Wanna Be With You/Every Time I Close My Eyes/Darlin'/Let's Have A Party/Roll With It/Nobody But You

'Backstreet Boys'
Released US: August 1997
Highest US chart position: 12
We've Got It Goin' On/Quit Playin' Games (With My Heart)/As Long As You Love Me/All I Have To Give/Anywhere For You/Hey Mr. DJ (Keep Playin' This Song)/I'll Never Break Your Heart/Darlin'/Get Down (You're The One For Me)/Set Adrift On Memory Bliss/If You Want It To Be Good Girl (Get Yourself A Bad Boy)

'Backstreet's Back'
Released UK: August 1997
Highest UK chart position: 2
Everybody (Backstreet's Back)/As Long As You Love Me/All I Have To Give/That's The Way I Like It/10,000 Promises/Like A Child/Hey Mr. DJ (Keep Playin' This Song)/Set Adrift On Memory Bliss/That's What She Said/If You Want It To Be Good Girl (Get Yourself A Bad Boy)/If I Don't Have You

Video

'Live In Concert'
Released UK: 1997
Let's Have A Party/End Of The Road/Just To Be Close To You/I'll Never Break Your Heart/Ain't Nobody (Instrumental)/I Wanna Be With You/ Anywhere For You/Darlin'/10,000 Promises/Boys Will Be Boys/Get Down (You're The One For Me)
